# A GOLFER'S NIGHT BEFORE Christmas

2005

Text
Jody Feldman

Illustrations
Shauna Mooney Kawasaki

GIBBS·SMITH
P
PUBLISHER

SALT LAKE CITY

To: Al
From: Kitty
BB Katz
Little Sweetie

07 06 05 04   13 12 11 10

Copyright ©1995 Gibbs Smith, Publisher

Printed in China
by Regent Publishing Services, Ltd.

Published by
Gibbs Smith, Publisher
P. O. Box 667
Layton, Utah 84041

ISBN 0-87905-682-7

'Twas the night
before Christmas.
With things
running fine,

Old Santa
decided
to play a
quick nine.

He packed up
his sleigh,
his clubs
well within reach;

then flew to a
good public
course near
the beach.

On the back nine,
a threesome
called out,
"Come and play.

"There's no one
behind us.
We're last
here today."

Santa smiled,
then teed up,
set his shoulder
blades square,

and took a
deep breath
from the
grass-scented air.

But he swung
much too hard
and in spite
of himself,

he took
up a divot
the size
of an elf.

If that
pitiful drive
wasn't lousy enough,

his fairway
shot found
a spot deep
in the rough.

Muttered he,
"Oh, perhaps,
it's the wrong
eve to play.

"I've more
meaningful deeds
to accomplish
today."

"Oh, no!"
they protested.
"That isn't
the thing.

"You just,
ever so slightly,
must alter
your swing."

The first man
stepped up.
"Change your grip.
Look alive.

"Swing faster,
but softer.
Now drive,
old man, drive!"

Santa swung
at the ball
with an air-splitting
THWACK!

But it popped up
and gave him
a smack
on the back.

The woman said,
"Santa,
now here's
what you do—

"Stand this way,
squint hard
then scream and
swing through."

Spoke the first guy,
"That tactic
went out
with the Edsels.

"You've got him
all twisted
like soft,
salted pretzels."

Santa swung,
nonetheless;
then he cried
out in pain.

"My back,"
he lamented,
"has gone out
again!"

Then a grizzled,
old gent
who'd a wisdom
like Snead did

gave Santa,
too late,
the advice he
had needed.

"You're out here
for fun,
and as you
grow calmer,

"you'll find yourself
hitting
like young
Arnold Palmer."

"But I can't
even move now."
The thought
made him shiver.

"I have all
these presents
I have
to deliver."

"Please help me
save Christmas.
Please give out
these toys."

Soon the foursome
flew off
to the good
girls and boys.

It was Santa
who now
gave out
tips to his crew,

as up in the air
past the rooftops
they flew.

At each home,
the golfers
found just
the right packs

and with magic
Yule dust
scooted down
chimney stacks.

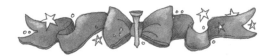

They twisted
and stretched
and got scorched
by Yule logs,

ate cookies
and milk
and got nipped
by some dogs.

But they said
as they passed
the last
fireplace screen,

"This is almost
as rousing
as playing eighteen!"

Santa said,
"You've done well,
and reward you,
I shall.

"We'll start at
St. Andrews,
Augusta,
Doral . . .

"We'll do lunch
in Scottsdale,
try Pebble Beach,
then,

"Riviera and
Sawgrass.
You just tell
me when.

"Then eleven
more holes—
what a dream round
we'll play!"

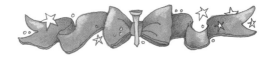

Then he took
the three home,
and he soon
flew away.

Soon they heard
him exclaim
from a sky dark
as slate,

"Merry Christmas
to all!
May your drives
all fly straight!"